TORONTO,
MAGNIFICENT CITY

Overlooking the city from the observation tower of the Canadian Imperial Bank of Commerce.

TORONTO

MAGNIFICENT CITY

An Illustrated Look at a Great Metropolis

by

Nick and Helma Mika

•

Mika Silk Screening Limited,

Belleville, Ont.

ACKNOWLEDGEMENTS

Our sincere thanks go to the following institutions, organizations and companies for supplying us with picture material and information which was used to compile this book:

Toronto Public Libraries, North York Public Library, Belleville Public Library;

York University, O'Keefe Centre for the Performing Arts, C.B.C. Television Network, CNE Publicity Dept., Old Mill Towers, Key to Toronto, Lansdowne Public School, Connaught Medical Research Laboratories.

The Globe and Mail, The Telegram, The Toronto Star;

The Toronto-Dominion Bank, The Bank of Nova Scotia, Canadian Imperial Bank of Commerce, The Bank of Montreal.

The Royal York, King Edward Sheraton, Park Plaza Hotel, Inn on the Park;

O'Keefe Brewing Co. Ltd., North American Life Assurance Co., Massey-Ferguson Ltd., Shell Canada Ltd., Moore Business Forms Ltd., The T. Eaton Co. Ltd., Heintzman & Co. Ltd., The Brown Brothers Ltd., Imperial Oil Ltd., The Consumer Gas Co., The Bell Telephone Co. of Canada, Bata Limited, Robert Simpson Co. Ltd., Honest Ed's Ltd., Canadian Pacific, Union Carbide Canada Ltd., Confederation Life Association.

Toronto Electric Commissioners, Board of Education for the City of Toronto, Toronto Transit Commission, The Toronto Harbour Commissioners, Department of Transport, City of Toronto Planning Board, Toronto Industrial Commission;

City of Toronto, The Municipality of Metropolitan Toronto, Metropolitan Toronto Industrial Commission.

WORKS CONSULTED:
J. Timperlake: Illustrated Toronto - 1877
Conyngham Crawford Taylor: Toronto "Called Back" - 1892
Robertson's Landmarks of Toronto - 1896
Jesse Edgar Middleton: The Municipality of Toronto - 1923
Jesse Edgar Middleton: Toronto's 100 Years - 1934
Edwin C. Guillet: Toronto Illustrated - 1939
Toronto Transport Commission: Wheels of Progress - 1953
Toronto '59 - compiled by B. T. Richardson - 1959
City of Toronto Planning Board: Plan for Downtown Toronto - 1963
City of Toronto: Municipal Handbook - 1965
Eric Arthur: Toronto no Mean City - 1965
Donald Kerr, Jacob Spelt; The Changing Face of Toronto - 1965
Metropolitan Toronto Industrial Commission: Toronto the exciting city - 1966

All colour illustrations were hand screened by Mika Studio, Belleville, Ontario.

Drawings for the illustrations were prepared from recent photographs taken by the authors, or from picture material kindly lent to us by the various institutions, companies and organizations mentioned above. The original drawings were made by:
Nick Mika, Harry Pollard, Robert Lott, John Berkhuizen, Jacob Berkhuizen and Gerry Putman.

CONTENTS

                                                    Page

Acknowledgements   4

Toronto Today   7

Living Past   47

A Glimpse into History   59

Of Enterprise and Prosperity   67

Places of Worship   95

The Mirrors of Toronto   101

From Steam Era to Jet Age   107

A Stroll through Toronto   115

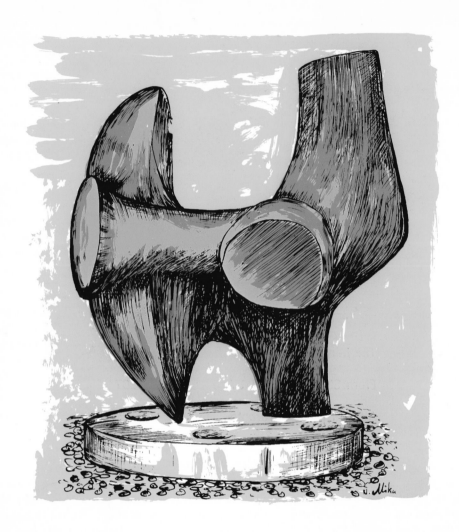

On the evening of October 27, 1966 Henry Moore's famous "Archer", a monumental abstract bronze sculpture, was unveiled in Toronto's Civic Square where it now stands in front of City Hall.

Toronto Today

To begin with I should tell you that I was not born in Toronto, and since I live a hundred miles away from the bustling metropolis, I am what you would call an outsider. To be honest, I am quite content not to have to worry about rush-hour traffic and whatever else people in big cities complain about. Come to think of it, the average Torontonian does not seem to do much complaining about his city. He is too busy planning the future, raising steel for gigantic structures or levelling ground for new super-speedways. Sure, he knows Toronto is not perfect, but if he criticizes his city, he does it with an air of confidence, knowing that eventually any problems will be solved. After all, he is helping to build the new Toronto, that is rapidly becoming one of the world's most fascinating cities. And he is proud of Toronto, very proud. As for me, I am slightly awed by the speed at which Toronto grows and changes. Now a community of nearly two million people, it attracts newcomers at the rate of close to ninety thousand a year gathering almost one quarter of Canada's immigrants into the Metropolitan fold.

There is no doubt that the Toronto of the 1960's is a magnificent, glittering city, but its future promises to be even more brilliant and exciting than the present. Dynamic plans and proposals for developments during the next two decades include more sweeping changes in the downtown area, scores of new highrise apartment and office buildings with spacious plazas and skywalks for pedestrians, elimination of eyesores and dilapidated houses, a vast extension of Metro's rapid transit and subway system, and a startling new face for Toronto's lakeshore and harbour.

Progress is a word which means "speed" in modern Toronto. It seems just yesterday that I took a streetcar along Bloor Street to the Colonnade. Today I stood for five minutes at the former stop on the corner of Yonge before I realized that the tracks had disappeared. A couple of quaint old houses that caught my eye just recently have since been swallowed up by an apartment complex which is "now renting". From the old bank building that once graced the corner of King and Bay Streets nothing is left but some of the beautiful stone sculptures which I understand are going to become museum pieces. In passing by I heard an oldtimer mumble "a sin to tear down that building". To-morrow he probably will be one of the sidewalk-superintendents watching a new ultra-modern banking pavilion rise in its place.

What I like most about Toronto, is the fact that it is full of variety and surprises. Next to a flamboyant, gleaming office block you may find an old dignified townhouse from the 1860's with a black iron fence and an elaborate gate. Within earshot of the busy Gardiner Expressway lies historic Fort York where the past of Toronto is kept alive while the skyscrapers of today are rising around it. Downtown, hidden behind ugly walls of warehouses, stands Holy Trinity Church just off Yonge Street, dating back to 1847. Overlooking the hustle and bustle of crowded streets in the heart of the city is a fairyland castle, one of North America's most unique tourist attractions. As you drive along a dreary street with second-hand clothing stores and bargain sale signs you suddenly discover a pleasant little park where old men are feeding pigeons and children are playing on the grass. Speaking of parks and gardens, Toronto has over two hundred, some of them with brilliant flower displays and trees older than the city itself. There are picnic areas, playing fields, swimming pools, skating rinks and tennis courts. Thickly wooded ravines are among the city's natural assets with trails for hiking and waterways for boating. Nowhere is there a sign to say "Keep off the Grass", not even on the beautifully kept grounds of the Canadian National Exhibition. High Park, a four hundred and twenty acre wooded estate in the centre of the city, is a gift from one of Toronto's early citizens to be enjoyed by generations to come.

Last week I accidentally discovered Kensington Market, a district just off Spadina between St. Andrews and Oxford Streets. Here you can select a live chicken, watch it being killed the kosher way, shop for exotic vegetables, a pair of shoes or a scatter rug or just wander from one stall to another along the crowded sidewalks. A Hungarian housewife is pushing a cart with a bushel basket full of paprikas, a Ukrainian woman is looking for fresh horse-radish, an old man is putting salt-herring in his shopping bag.

Walking along the southern part of Spadina you likely hear any language except English. As far as food is concerned, on Spadina you can eat kosher, spicy, Polish or German, and you find anything from bagels to Knockwurst and Knishes. There are just as many churches of different denominations along this stretch of Spadina and its sidestreets as there are people of various backgrounds. Spadina Avenue seems to have lured the immigrants since the turn of the century. It is the street where thousands of them have set up house and shop and carried on their old traditions. First it was a Jewish community, then came Ukrainians and Italians, and by the 1950's most newcomers to Toronto had heard of Spadina if nothing else. It was here that they felt at home in a strange land. Teaming with activities as varied as its people, Spadina now has become the hub of a huge garment industry and has the reputation of being the most colourful street in Toronto, if not in all of Canada.

If you like Bohemian atmosphere, come with me to Yorkville where stores and restaurants have such unconventional names as "The Cat's Meow" or "The Walrus and the Carpenter". The hairstyles featured by some of Yorkville's younger male residents are a curiosity in themselves, and if it were not for the present mini-skirt fad with the girls, one might easily get confused. Being past the discothèque-generation, I prefer to sit on the terrace of the "Penny Farthing" sipping one of the milder versions of their Espresso concoctions and listening to the strings of a guitar. To my regret, the last time I went to the Penny Farthing the colour of the building had changed from vivid purple to just plain white. Somehow the purple had been more in keeping with the atmosphere of the Village as Yorkville is sometimes called.

A shopping spree in Toronto can be an adventure all its own. All you need is some subway tickets to cover the distances, a pair of good feet to wander around the rows of stores, a walletful of money or credit cards, and you can have the time of your life. There are Eaton's and Simpson's lavish department stores with merchandise from every corner of the globe, the elegant shops on Bloor Street, also called Toronto's Fifth Avenue, and the Colonnade, a collection of exquisite boutiques, restaurants, offices, penthouses and a theatre, all under one single roof. On Bloor Street West is Honest Ed's unique discount store, a paradise for bargain hunters and busy as a bee-hive with uniformed guards keeping the inside traffic under control. Stepping out of Honest Ed's onto Markham Street, you are in the peaceful surroundings of Markham Village, a block of quaint, gaily painted houses with gingerbread trim, sidewalk cafés, boutiques, tearooms and antique shops. Among the more than 140 shopping plazas in the Metropolitan area, Yorkdale claims the fame of being the largest enclosed shopping centre in the world. With climate-controlled malls and over a hundred fashionable stores, taverns, restaurants, service establishments and a theatre, it is almost a small town in itself.

As for variety in entertainment, Toronto today offers a choice second to none. There is the ultra-modern O'Keefe Centre featuring the best in shows and talents. The Royal Alexandra, once Toronto's leading legitimate theatre, still attracts famous names of show business on its stage. At present Toronto has eighteen live theatres and eighty movie houses. As an employer of entertainment talent, Toronto follows directly behind New York. The Toronto Symphony Orchestra has gained world renown. The National Ballet is part of the Toronto scene. So are the night clubs, gourmet restaurants and off-beat coffeehouses. Whether you like jazz or folk songs, opera or Dixie music, you are sure to find it in Toronto. If you are a spectator sportsman, Toronto is the place to be. Home of the Maple Leafs, Toronto's Maple Leaf Gardens are the Mecca for every hockey fan in a hundred-mile radius on Saturday night.

There are times when I ponder the possibility of coming to Toronto to live. Twenty years ago that thought might not have occurred to me. Sure, Toronto was a clean, pleasant city with plenty of opportunity, but the truth is that in those days it seemed rather dull compared to some of the European cities I knew. Today Toronto has changed. So much so, that I now find it hard to resist its magic lure, the lure of a vigorous Metropolis that hums with a thousand activities, spreads out over an area of two hundred and forty square miles and builds its buildings tall and luxurious. In the last two decades Toronto has emerged as one of the most lively and progressive urban centres and has taken its place among the greatest cities in the world. Once predominantly Anglo-Saxon, Metro citizens today hail from every country on the earth. Immigrants who came in large numbers after the last war brought with them their countless skills, their customs and cultures, their hopes and dreams. By preserving their ethnic heritage they enhanced the Toronto scene, and while some of them created their own distinct communities within the great metropolis, they live in perfect harmony with the so-called old Torontonians and share a common pride in the new city they are helping to shape. Today Toronto has the unique appeal of a city that blends traditions and virtues of the past with modern concepts and twentieth century drive and efficiency.

Speaking of efficiency, Toronto's transportation system is one of its most marvellous wonders. Streetcars, buses, subways, highways, express and speedways carry a never diminishing volume of passengers, cars and vehicles of every description with un-believable speed across and around the vast metropolitan area. Traffic jams occur relatively seldom, unless, of course, you happen to get stuck in one. Toronto now, incidentally, is the only city in Canada where you can still ride on a streetcar, although its days may be numbered. The public transit system on the surface alone covers nearly five hundred miles. Toronto's subway trains are modern, speedy and comfortable. The Yonge Street route was the first to be built in Canada. It carries up to forty thousand passengers in one direction per hour. The newly opened Bloor-Danforth-University subway handles one third of a million passengers a day; it cost two hundred million dollars to build. When two more extensions to the subway system will be completed in 1967, passengers will be able to cover the distance of fourteen miles across town from Warden Avenue in Scarborough to Islington Avenue in Etobicoke in less than half an hour.

Occasionally I get confused in the tangle of new speed and expressways that seem to soar straight up into the sky or fan out like the legs of a giant octopus. Once or twice I found myself miles away from where I intended to go. But you don't have to be from out of town to get into this kind of predicament, so I am told by Torontonians.

Toronto has more churches than most cities I know, but the Sundays are gone when, according to the oldtimers, you could shoot a cannon up Yonge Street without hitting anyone. Not so long ago Toronto used to be notorious for its dreary Sundays, when the only public doors open were those of its churches. Once the city was known as Toronto, the Good. Today it is Toronto, the Exciting. One of the reasons it has become such a lively, swinging city is the fact that nearly one third of its population at present is under twenty years of age. The spirit of Toronto in the 1960's is young and gay.

And Toronto is prosperous, immensely prosperous. As the industrial centre of Ontario whose capital it became in 1867, Toronto is a place where big business is transacted, where the headquarters of major companies are located and far-reaching decisions are made. Within a hundred mile radius of Toronto is concentrated nearly one third of Canada's buying power. On Bay Street, in the heart of the city's financial district, operates one of North America's busiest stock exchanges with a trading volume second only to that of the New York Exchange. With the construction of the St. Lawrence Seaway Toronto has become an inland ocean port open to the world's markets. Its bustling harbour which annually handles close to six million tons of cargo, its humming railway freight yards that load an average of twelve thousand cars per month, its international airport that sees three million passengers arrive and depart in a year, its traffic arteries that carry an endless flow of truck loads to and from the city, they all reflect progress and prosperity. So do the giant investment and trust company buildings, the stock, bond and brokerage houses and the elaborate edifices of old established banks. Toronto's ever-changing skyline is dotted with construction cranes promising a new crop of factories, office and apartment buildings for to-morrow. The dollar value of building permits issued in Toronto in recent years has only been topped on the North American continent by two cities, New York and Los Angeles.

Toronto's planners and businessmen are thinking big. Some of their ambitious re-development programs are measured not in hundred thousands but in hundred millions. Nearing completion now is the tallest skyscraper in the Commonwealth, a fifty-six storey tower which is part of the 125,000,000 dollar Toronto-Dominion Centre that will cover four acres of open space and will include a forty-four storey tower as well as an elegant banking pavilion. The T. Eaton Company plans a 250,000,000 dollar project that will drastically change the face of more than twenty acres of downtown area, eradicate dismal warehouses and blight, and turn them into a complex more lavish than Rockefeller Centre. Rising at the corner of Queen and Bay Streets is the thirty-three storey Robert Simpson Tower being erected at a cost of more than fourteen million dollars. Gigantic lakefront developments will create a new skyline, adding scores of buildings and facilities needed in a community bursting at its seams. Suburbs too are planning vigorously and big, reaching toward the sky. Highrise construction is dominating today's building boom. And wherever you look, Toronto is building.

Needless to say, that in the process of renewing itself Toronto has to make sacrifices. As a city that looks to the future it cannot often afford nostalgic memories. Some of the old familiar landmarks must disappear. Buildings that weathered a century have to be demolished and will live only on the pages of history books. Colourful Chinatown already has lost its southern section, and what is left may not be there for long. Sunnyside Amusement Park made way for the six-lane Gardiner Expressway and the waterfront development. The days of the majestic old City Hall are counted.

Today Toronto possesses a new City Hall that is not only one of the most striking contemporary buildings in the world, but also one of the boldest and most unusual. Set on a large Civic Square with wide open spaces its slender, curving towers have become the symbol of Toronto's spirit, magnificent and adventurous.

Toronto today is a blend of many things. As an outsider I do not concern myself with any of its shortcomings, I merely enjoy its beauty. It would take years to explore Toronto and you would still not see it all. But come along with me and take a glimpse at Canada's most fascinating city.

The New City Hall

Unique and daring in concept, Toronto's new City Hall was designed by Finnish architect Viljo Revell who did not live to see his masterpiece completed. As the curving towers

13

began to rise, he called it his greatest triumph. To the world it has become one of the most talked-about and admired contemporary buildings. Two slender towers, slightly concave, are flanking a mushroom-shaped central building which contains a circular council chamber and the mayor's offices. Set on a large civic square which replaces thirteen acres of once dismal, uninspiring clutter with fountains, walks, trees and a reflecting pool that becomes an open-air skating rink in the winter, the new City Hall is now the focal point of Metropolitan Toronto. Around it plans of gigantic proportions are beginning to reshape the core of the city, promising skywalks, theatres, ultra-modern apartments and elegant office buildings. The new City Hall has become Toronto's proudest achievement and an inspiration for the future.

University Avenue looking north

University Avenue, unusually wide and lined with impressive edifices on either side, is Toronto's boulevard of prestige. A centre strip of well-groomed lawns and fountains separates the flow of traffic as it leads to Queen's Park with a full view of the Parliament Buildings.

Bay Street looking north toward old City Hall Tower

In the narrow canyon of downtown Bay Street beats the financial heart of a city that now is the business capital of Canada.

Skyline at night

Toronto's ever changing skyline tells the story of a city alive with ambition, a city where construction projects are not only immense but more numerous than anywhere else on this continent. Buildings along the waterfront are growing taller as Toronto, bursting at its seams, is reaching skyward. The 740-foot Toronto-Dominion Tower can be seen for nearly thirty miles. At night the sky seems ablaze with a million lights and people take the ferry to the island to enjoy the spectacle. A few years from now the Toronto skyline will have changed again, as a gigantic new waterfront development begins to take shape and mark the outlines of the ever growing metropolis.

The Old City Hall

Still a stately landmark of Toronto is the slender 300-foot clock tower of the old City Hall. Its red sandstone blackened by time, its Victorian elegance undiminished, it is a striking contrast to its more flamboyant successor. When it was being built to replace the first town hall on Front Street, the city's population had grown to two hundred thousand. The story goes that repeated construction delays and frustrating squabbles caused the Mayor one day to pick up his chair during a council meeting, and, followed by some of the aldermen, he went to Queen Street and continued the meeting in the half-finished new council chamber, watched by bewildered carpenters and painters. The official opening took place on September 18, 1899, as Mayor John Shaw and his councillors arrived in two streetcars drawn by twelve grey horses each, and unlocked the door with a golden key. During sixty-six eventful years the old City Hall tower watched Toronto expand and change into a great, bustling metropolis, and its powerful bells have rung out the hours since New Year's Eve at the turn of the century.

Monument of Governor Simcoe in Queen's Park

In 1793 John Graves Simcoe, first Lieutenant-Governor of Upper Canada, began to build a fort on the shore of Lake Ontario at the entrance of Toronto Bay. He called the fort "York" after the son of George III and transferred the seat of government to the tiny settlement which was destined to become the Toronto we know today.

Parliament Buildings

Ontario's first Parliament Buildings dating back to the year 1796 once stood at the corner of what is now Front and Berkeley Streets. After they were burned to the ground by American attackers during the war of 1812, a new brick building was put up at the same site in 1818, but eventually it too was gutted by fire. West of the present Union Station on Front Street was the location of a third and more elaborate building which served as the seat of government until on April 4, 1893 the Ontario Legislature opened its 26th session under Premier Sir Oliver Mowat at the new Parliament Buildings situated in Queen's Park at the head of University Avenue.

Maple Leaf Gardens

Maple Leaf Gardens, a colossal building at Church and Carlton Streets, is known the world over to hockey fans as one of the most famous ice hockey rinks. Home of the Toronto Maple Leafs, the team which many times brought home the coveted Stanley Cup, the Gardens are host to nearly fifteen thousand spectators on hockey nights in Canada, and not a single seat is vacant. Since the Gardens opened during the beginning of the depression years, they have been the scene of many great rallies, community events and hundreds of thrilling hockey games.

The new Woodbine Race Track

A short distance from the city, just off Highway 27 near Malton Airport, the new Woodbine Race Track spreads out over an area of seven hundred and eighty acres. Here the excitement of playing the horses is matched by the grandeur of the largest and most modern race track in North America. Opened in 1956, the new Woodbine track can accommodate over forty thousand spectators, nine thousand of them seated on the grandstand which is built high in order to give everyone a clear view of the finish line. Incidentally, the old Woodbine Track, dating back to 1874 and situated in the east end of the city, is now known as Greenwood Race Track.

Casa Loma

N. Mika

A hundred rooms filled with splendour and lavish extravaganza, twenty-three fireplaces, secret passages between floors, a stable lined with marble and mahogany, and a wine cellar holding over eighteen hundred bottles, those are only some of the luxuries on which Sir Henry Pellatt squandered his fortune when he built Casa Loma. But his fondest dream, that of entertaining royalty in his castle, never came true.

Medieval in appearance, a mixture of architectural styles and whimsical notions, Casa Loma is certainly one of the most unusual castles in the world and one of the few to be found in North America. Not only did it cost Sir Henry three million dollars to build his "House on the Hill" on a six-acre estate in the heart of the city, it also ruined him financially. Today Casa Loma has become one of Toronto's biggest tourist attractions.

Built to commemorate the visit of the Prince of Wales and the Duke of Kent to Toronto in 1927, Princes' Gate is the impressive main entrance to Toronto's beautifully landscaped Exhibition Park, an area of three hundred and fifty acres stretching for a mile and a half along the shore of Lake Ontario. Home of the famous Canadian National Exhibition, the largest annual fair in the world, the park is host to three million visitors during the three weeks of this "Greatest Show on Earth". Another estimated three million people yearly attend conventions, trade shows and such events as the Royal Winter Fair, held in the permanent buildings of the park.

Princes' Gate

23

Massey Music Hall on Shuter and Victoria Streets first opened its doors to the public on June 14, 1894 with a music festival under the direction of Dr. Torrington. Intended to serve the city solely as a music centre, the building was erected by Hart A. Massey, member of a well-known, public-spirited family. In its long history Massey Hall has been a great temple of musical art and has become synonymous with unforgettable performances. The excellent acoustics of Massey Hall are known to be unequalled by any other concert hall in North America. As the home of the Toronto Symphony Orchestra, whose fame has spread throughout the world, Massey Hall now as in the past offers the best in music and audiences are crowding the auditorium to hear concert artists of international acclaim.

Massey Hall

On October 1, 1960, the ultra-modern, multi-million dollar O'Keefe Centre opened with the world premiere of "Camelot". Since then it has become one of Canada's foremost theatres and a showcase for some of the world's great talents. Situated at Front and Yonge Streets, the striking, graceful building was the result of five years planning and construction. As a centre for the performing arts it is dedicated to the presentation of classic and contemporary theatre and offers drama, opera, musical comedy, symphony and ballet.

The auditorium has a seating capacity for 3,200 which can be reduced to a more intimate theatre for 1,100 by drawing an acoustic curtain in front of the balcony. The stage area extends across 128 feet of the building. Remote-controlled stage lighting, a mechanically elevated 50-piece orchestra pit, electronically amplified sound and unique acoustic facilities, those are only some of the most up-to-date features the O'Keefe Centre offers its patrons.

O'Keefe Centre

Royal Alexandra Theatre

When the Royal Alexandra Theatre opened its doors on August 26, 1907 with the musical "Top of the World", it began an era that was to see it become Toronto's leading legitimate theatre. It was built by millionaire-businessman Cawthra Mulock. Some fifty years later, its baroque splendour beginning to show the wear and tear of time, it was bought by Edwin Mirvish, another wealthy Toronto businessman and patron of the arts. He equipped the theatre with modern stage facilities and restored it to its original lavish beauty at the cost of half a million dollars and gave it a new lease on life.

The Colonnade

The Colonnade on Bloor Street West is a shopper's delight with a host of specialty shops and boutiques, all under one roof. The building also contains restaurants, a legitimate theatre, offices, studios and penthouses.

Yorkville Village

Jazz, folk songs, discothèques, coffee houses, fashionable couturiers and shops, that is Yorkville, Toronto's version of Greenwich Village. A small two-block area between Bay Street and Avenue Road just off Bloor Street, it is the centre of Bohemian life, a tourist attraction for thousands and an exciting place for a night out in Toronto. The Village has many faces. In the daytime it is sidewalk cafés, quaint gingerbread houses, restaurants and shops with far-out names, bare-footed girls with straggly hair in mini-skirts sitting, listless, on the doorstep, clusters of boys hanging around, sporting iron crosses, long hair and high-heeled boots. A newcomer with a knapsack full of his worldly belongings on his back arrives to join the ranks of youngsters who defy society's way of life, a nameless drifter drawn to Yorkville from a far away place. At night the Village changes. As the scene shifts indoors, the youngsters are "switched on", some by drugs, other by the beat of drums. A throng of visitors takes over the street, milling about, and Yorkville's nightlife begins.

28

Markham Village

If you like a picturesque neighbourhood, take a stroll through Markham Village, where Edwin Mirvish, the owner of Honest Ed's famous cut-rate store, transformed a row of old dilapidated houses with a splash of bright pastel colours and a touch of genius into one of Toronto's most unique attractions.

Just south of his store on Markham and Bloor, he created an artist colony with curio shops, art studios, coffeehouses and tables along the sidewalk. Here you can eat French Onion Soup, delicious and piping hot, served in the summer right outside underneath an old iron soup kettle dangling from the roof of the porch. "Come, take a peek at my boutique", says one sign in the window, "Tea Cup Reading" is offered by another. Handicraft and exquisite gifts, stores with names like "The Man Trap", spinning wheels and antique furniture sitting neatly arranged on the pavement, a carved painted totem pole placed in front of a bright yellow house, people taking it easy - that is the atmosphere of Markham Village.

Gooderham Building

At Front and Wellington Streets in a neighbourhood that saw much of Toronto's early history still stands an old landmark. It is the rather unusual looking, pie-shaped Gooderham building dating back to 1892. Now seemingly out of place in the midst of modern traffic which swirls around it, the building is associated with the name of an old Toronto family. The Gooderhams not only were financiers but well-known distillers under the name of Gooderham and Worts. Across the street from the Gooderham building, at the corner of Wellington and Church, was once the site of the famous Ontario House, a popular hotel built around 1832 and later known as the Wellington Hotel. Newspaper advertisements in the old days described it as having, among other advantages, "large double beds kept free from vermin and insects of any kind". Until the early 1900's the historic corner was occupied by the old Bank of Toronto which the Gooderham family helped to found.

Yonge Street is one of the oldest and most historic streets in Toronto. It started out as a trail cut through the wilderness by Governor Simcoe's soldiers in 1795. As a link between the small settlement of York and Lake Simcoe it was once used by fur traders and trappers. The town's first industry opened on Yonge Street in 1812, when Jesse Ketchum started tanning hides at a site where is now the corner of Yonge and Adelaide Streets. In 1849 Yonge Street was the route of the city's first public transportation service, a horse-drawn omnibus operated by a cabinetmaker between the St. Lawrence Market and the Red Lion Hotel at Yorkville. By 1861 a horse-drawn street railway, the first in Canada, ambled along Yonge Street. In 1869 Timothy Eaton established his first modest dry goods store on Yonge, and Robert Simpson opened his store on the same street three years later. A business street and one of the liveliest thoroughfares Yonge has been ever since.

31

Queen Street

When Toronto still was called the village of York in the early part of the nineteenth century, Queen Street ran along its northern boundary. It was known as Lot Street then until 1842 when its name was changed in honour of Queen Victoria. In its days Queen Street has seen fashionable residences, prosperous business establishments as well as decaying rows of drab tenements. One stretch of Queen Street runs along the southern edge of what is known as Cabbagetown, once a pretty district where Irish settlers planted cabbages instead of grass in front of their neat little houses, later a name associated with skid row and slums. Some of Queen Street's once elegant sections are now second-hand clothing and furniture stores, dilapidated warehouses, peeling paint and sagging verandahs. To-morrow these houses may be changing hands, and some years from now skyscrapers may be taking their places.

Juvenile and Family Court Building, Jarvis Street

33

The New Court House

Metro's recently completed seven-storey court house has joined the monumental new landmarks of the downtown area. A mall connects the new court house with historic Osgoode Hall, seat of the Supreme Court of Ontario. The ultra-modern fourteen million dollar building was erected on the site of the old University Avenue Armories, and its windowless, air-conditioned, spacious court rooms are a far cry from the cramped, antiquated quarters formerly occupied in the old city hall.

Osgoode Hall

Osgoode Hall, home of the Law Society of Upper Canada and seat of the Supreme Court of Ontario, was named after William Osgoode who became the first Chief Justice of Upper Canada in 1792. Situated on Queen Street at University Avenue, the building was begun in 1829 and was standing then outside the city limits. A wooden walk led to its doors in the old days. A high wrought-iron fence still surrounds the grounds. The elaborate cow gates were designed to keep stray cattle from grazing on the well-kept lawns. With its later additions and alterations, Osgoode Hall is now grouped among the oldest historic public buildings in the city and is considered a perfect example of classic architecture in Canada.

The main entrance to University College with its rich and intricate detail is in itself a work of beauty and perfection. It has been called a showpiece of Norman architecture, revived in the Romanesque style of a later century. The door is placed in the massive centre tower which dominates the building and leads into an elaborately finished entrance hall.

Main Entrance to University College

University College is one of the oldest buildings on the campus of the University of Toronto. Dating back to the year 1856, it is considered an excellent example of Romanesque style blended with Gothic elements. Now the non-denominational arts college of the University of Toronto and one of nearly a hundred buildings on the main campus, it once accommodated the entire student body of the University. Fire gutted the east wing including the museum and the 33,000-volume library on the night of February 14, 1890 when a servant stumbled and upset a kerosene lamp. Although insurance covered less than half of the disastrous loss, University College soon rose again from the ashes and was restored to its original splendour.

University College

Hart House

Situated north-east of University College is a Tudor-style building known as Hart House. It was given to the University of Toronto by the Massey Foundation and named after Hart Massey, leading manufacturer and philanthropist. The Gothic tower at the west end is known as the Soldier's Tower. It was built as a memorial to students and graduates who sacrificed their lives for their country in two great wars.

York University was founded in 1959. Its first students, numbering less than one hundred, were enrolled at Falconer Hall on the University of Toronto campus. Now there is Glendon campus at Bayview and Lawrence Avenues with a small residential liberal arts college limited to one thousand students, Atkinson College which offers all its degree courses and instructions in the evening, and the new 472-acre York campus on Keele Street south of Steeles Avenue which was opened in 1965. It is estimated that by 1980 York campus alone will have a student population of seventeen thousand. A continuous construction program now underway will span the next two decades and its cost will be around the one hundred million dollar mark.

39

R.Lott

Scarborough College

Scarborough College, the newest addition to the University of Toronto, is situated twenty miles from the main campus on the brow of a hill overlooking a ravine. As the unique, unconventional structure began to take shape, it was compared by some critics to an ancient fortress, by others to an Egyptian pyramid. Some people simply called it a "happening". To say the least, at first glance, the massive building with the towering triple chimneys of the humanities wing is overwhelming. It is totally different and as far removed from the traditional college style as the electronic era from the middle ages. Actually, the structure was designed around television installations and the planners' first concern was to adapt the building to its functions. Relatively small labs and lecture rooms are equipped with visual aid facilities and closed circuit television. Scarborough College, ultra-modern in every respect, is not only a place for higher learning, but a landmark of Metropolitan Toronto.

The Archives Building of the Province of Ontario

Four famous figures of Canadian history, cut in stone, adorn the front façade of the Provincial Archives Building in Queen's Park. They are Samuel Champlain, General Wolfe, Governor Simcoe and General Brock. The building houses the archives of the Province of Ontario which preserve official documents and records as well as private papers and journals which relate to the history of the province. Also located in the building is the Sigmund Samuel Canadiana Gallery, a valuable collection of historic prints and paintings.

41

Lansdowne Public School on Robert Street is a striking example of contemporary school architecture. Being not only functional but also attractive, the building helps to enhance its surroundings and is a far cry from its outmoded predecessor which was torn down in 1961 after serving for three quarters of a century. A huge boulder sitting on the grounds was found during excavating for the new school and a plaque tells that it might have been carried there from Caribou Lake by a glacier about twelve thousand years ago.

42

The Royal Ontario Museum can claim to be the world's largest and one of the most fascinating of university museums. The present building, located south of Bloor Street at the intersection of Queen's Park, opened its doors to the public in 1933. Since then the museum has gained the reputation of having among its more than one million catalogued possessions the finest collection of ancient Chinese art to be found anywhere in the western world. Among the many unique attractions are the tomb of the Chinese Emperor in the museum garden, a massive totem pole over eighty feet tall inside the main hall, extensive exhibits depicting Eskimo and Indian life, and an impressive array of weapons and armour used by man throughout the centuries. The vast galleries and wings of the museum's four floors are filled with priceless treasures and reminders of the past recording the evolution of nature and man.

Gooderham and FitzGerald Buildings of the Connaught Medical Research Laboratories

Relentless research in the field of medical science, preparation of serums, vaccines and other substances of importance in preventive medicine have been the major projects of the Connaught Medical Research Laboratories ever since their beginnings more than half a century ago. Over the years their devoted scientists have tried to conquer suffering and disease, and with their brilliant discoveries have made medical history. Production of Insulin, Typhus Vaccine and Penicillin, preparation of fractions of human blood, research which contributed to the development of Salk Vaccine, these are only some of the varied activities of the Laboratories. In order to consolidate the work of their Spadina and College Divisions the Laboratories moved most of their operations to new and modern quarters on Steeles Avenue West in the summer of 1966.

Toronto's school system has come a long way since the first state school opened in 1807 at the corner of King and George Streets. In the early days education was the

The Education Centre

privilege of children whose parents could afford to pay the required fees and support was given to grammar schools and universities rather than to the so-called common or public schools. Free, publicly supported schools for all children did not become a reality until the middle of the nineteenth century when a new educational system came into effect. 1850 was the year when the first school board was elected by the people of Toronto. In the more than a century of its history the board's work and responsibilities have grown with new concepts of education and the number of schools and pupils in the

45

city which it is serving. In 1958 construction was begun on a combined administration building and education centre. Located on College Street, the centre now houses many departments, once scattered throughout the city, provides a meeting place for teachers and educational organizations and, with its modern facilities, promotes advanced educational practices.

Living Past

Among the landmarks of a city are those that tourist guides list as "places of historic interest". They are part of a living heritage preserved for generations to come. They tell about the early life of a city and its people, and each reflects a slice of history. Unfortunately, not many of these buildings are left in Toronto. Some fell victim of neglect, others were demolished to make way for progress. But those that have survived are now treasured possessions, and within their walls lives the past.

There is Old Fort York, Toronto's most significant historic site at the foot of Bathurst Street and situated a stone's throw from the Gardiner Expressway that walks on stilts across the roof tops of downtown Toronto. The fort was established in 1793 by Governor Simcoe to defend the settlement of York which he had chosen as the site of Upper Canada's capital.

During the Battle of York in 1813, at the height of the American War, the fort was captured and temporarily held by American forces. Their commander, General Pike, was killed. His soldiers sacked the town, burned public buildings and carried off the parliamentary mace. It was in reprisal for the burning of York that British troops eventually burned public buildings in Washington and set fire to the President's mansion. Over a

Old Fort York

century later, in 1934 to be exact, when Toronto celebrated its centennial as a city, President Franklin D. Roosevelt returned the Upper Canada Mace to the Ontario Government. It is now among the exhibits at Fort York.

Restored to what it was in bygone days, Fort York consists of soldiers' barracks, officers' quarters and powder magazines. Two of the blockhouses date back to the year 1813. One of the old bronze cannons of the fort is fired daily during the summer months. Soldiers in the uniforms of the old garrison, exhibits and displays, rooms furnished as they were one hundred and fifty years ago, they all tell visitors the story of the early days of York.

Scadding Cabin

Toronto's oldest existing home is a humble pioneer cottage now standing in Exhibition Park near the very spot where once a French trading post flourished and Fort Rouille, also known as Fort Toronto, was built by the French in 1750. Originally, the log cabin stood on the east bank of the Don River just outside the limits of York. John Scadding, an English immigrant who came with John Graves Simcoe to Upper Canada, built it in 1794 as his first homestead. Years later, when he had become prosperous, he sold the cottage and moved his family to a more spacious home. Scadding's son Henry, incidentally, became Toronto's first historian.

The little cabin might well have been lost as an authentic relic from the pioneer days, had it not been for the members of the York Pioneer and Historical Society who in 1879 moved it by oxcart to its present location. Furnished in the manner of distant and more rugged days, Scadding Cabin ever since has been a living reminder of Toronto's past.

Mackenzie House

A colourful politician and fiery patriot, a sharp-tongued journalist and publisher, a many times elected and often expelled member of the Legislative Assembly, chief organizer of the 1837 Rebellion in Upper Canada, William Lyon Mackenzie was also the first mayor of the City of Toronto. He came to Canada from Scotland in 1820 and began his many careers as a shopkeeper in York selling drugs and books. The last years of his life he lived in the now historic house at 82 Bond Street where he died on August 28, 1861.

The Grange

Among the fine old houses preserved in their dignified beauty and untouched by the passing of time is the Grange, a grand mansion behind the Art Gallery of Toronto. The two-storey main structure, built of hand-made brick and black walnut in modified Georgian style with neo-classic touches, dates back to the year 1817. Wings and a conservatory were added later. For many years the Grange, surrounded by a 100-acre park, was the residence of the Boulton family. The Boultons loved to entertain and their house was the scene of many an elegant ball and dinner party. A private race track on the grounds provided exciting entertainment fare. Among the prominent guests was Lord Elgin, Governor-General of Canada, who on occasion used the Grange as his residence at the invitation of Toronto's mayor, William Henry Boulton. Today the Grange is part of the Art Gallery of Toronto.

St. Lawrence Hall

The first public market in the town of York was established by proclamation in 1803. To this day, still at its original site, St. Lawrence Market comes to life every Saturday when market gardeners bring their produce and shoppers crowd the stalls. Still presiding over the market place is St. Lawrence Hall, dating back to 1850. Once a building of elegance and prestige, it used to be the centre of civic events, concerts, banquets and balls. It was here that the Swedish Nightingale, Jenny Lind, gave two concerts that conquered the hearts of Toronto.

Colborne Lodge

Overlooking Lake Ontario from a hilltop in High Park, Colborne Lodge was once the country home of John George Howard, engineer, architect and the city's first appointed surveyor. It was Mr. Howard who designed St. James Cemetery, surveyed Toronto's harbour, constructed the sewers and laid down the first plank sidewalks on King Street. From his drawing board came many of Toronto's buildings in the last century. His Regency-style cottage he built in 1836 and named it after Lieutenant-Governor Colborne. Not far from it he later erected a cairn of granite boulders, and there, underneath the old trees, he and his wife are buried. High Park which he loved he bequeathed to the city as a public park, and his house is now maintained as a museum of early Canadiana. In it the visitor finds many of Mr. Howard's own paintings depicting the Toronto of his day when there were neither automobiles nor diesel engines and he could see from his window the puffing woodburners of the Grand Trunk Railway pull the trains along the lake shore down below.

Marine Museum of Upper Canada

The rather plain and austere looking building in Exhibition Park which now houses the Marine Museum of Upper Canada, was once part of the so-called New Fort. Built in 1841, it then served as officers' quarters for the British military establishment. In 1893 it was named Stanley Barracks in honour of Lord Stanley, Governor-General of Canada. Today the historic building contains exhibits that tell the story of the exploration of central Canada and the development of shipping on the inland waterways. Among the models on display are Eskimo kayaks, primitive birch-bark canoes, Great Lake steamers, passenger vessels and freighters that once sailed the inland seas of Canada.

No. 10 Toronto Street

The elegant, temple-like structure, now simply known as No. 10 Toronto Street, was built in 1853 as the city's seventh post office. To this day it has been preserved by its present owners as a symbol of nineteenth century prosperity and a pleasing change of scenery in the midst of rising skyscrapers.

Bank of Montreal, Front and Yonge Streets

A striking contrast to contemporary architecture, the magnificent stone structure of the Bank of Montreal at the corner of Front and Yonge Streets dates back to the year 1885. The beauty of its richly sculptured facade is matched by its elaborate interior. Until 1949 the building served as the bank's main office in Toronto.

ARMS OF THE CITY OF TORONTO

Armorial Bearings

ARMS: Quarterly gules and azure a cross argent charged in the centre point with a maple leaf gules veined or in the first quarter three lions passant gardant in pale or in the second a rose argent barbed and seeded proper in the third a cogwheel argent and in the fourth quarter on a base wavy barry wavy or and gules a presentation of the paddle steamer "Great Britain" under full steam and with pennon and flags flying all gold.

CREST: On a mural crown or a beaver proper.

SUPPORTERS: On the dexter side a Mississauga Indian habited and accoutred and supporting in the dexter hand a bow and on the sinister side a female figure representing Britannia all proper.

MOTTO: Industry, Intelligence, Integrity.

Registered with College of Arms, London, England, December 20, 1961.

DESCRIPTION OF ARMORIAL BEARINGS

The Arms, Crest and Supporters have their own emblematic meanings which are given for information.

The first quarter of the shield contains the lions of the Royal Arms of England. The Royal Arms flew over Old Fort York at the time of the War of 1812 and this occasioned York to be known quite frequently as Royal York. They have been a permanent feature of the City's Arms ever since. Special dispensation from Her Majesty Queen Elizabeth II enabled the continued use of this device as, normally, its use is not allowed in Coats of Arms.

The White Rose of York shown in the second quarter of the shield is emblematic of the origin of Toronto as the Town of York.

In the third quarter symbolizing the industrial stature of Toronto is a cogwheel.

The steamboat, representing the paddle steamer "Great Britain", which plied Lake Ontario in the 1830's and was a frequent visitor to the harbour at York, portrays the eminence of Toronto both as a world port and as a centre of Commerce.

The central placing of the Maple Leaf symbolizes Toronto as the Capital of the Province of Ontario.

A Mississauga Indian is the dexter supporter. This figure represents the early inhabitants of the area upon which the City of Toronto has grown. The sinister supporter is a female figure representing Britannia and is indicative of the bonds between Canada and Britain.

The mural crown of the Crest is shown composed of Masonry. This device is frequently used in English cities as a Corporation symbol.

The beaver is intended to depict both the Canadian identity of Toronto and industry.

ARMS OF THE CITY OF TORONTO

A Glimpse into History

A trading post in the wilderness, that was Toronto two centuries ago. In 1793 Governor Simcoe chose it as the capital of Upper Canada before even a settlement had been established.

The first white man to set foot on the land where Toronto now stands was Etienne Brûlé who visited the area in 1615.

Long known to the French as the Toronto Carrying Place, an Indian trail led from the mouth of the Humber River north to Lake Simcoe. To protect the rich fur trade in the region, the French established a fortified post in 1750 at the foot of what is now Dufferin Street. Although they named it Fort Rouille after the French colonial minister,

Fort Rouille - 1750

Obelisk in Exhibition Park

it was more often referred to as Fort Toronto, a name applied by the Huron Indians to the area. It means "Place of Meeting". Nine years later Fort Toronto was ordered to be burned by its own commandant to prevent its use by the British, and the French garrison withdrew to Montreal. Of the once flourishing trading post nothing remains today but an obelisk erected at the actual site which is now part of the Exhibition grounds.

And then came the famous Toronto Purchase. It was in 1787 when the British purchased from the Indians the land on which the city now stands. The price for an area stretching fourteen miles along Lake Ontario and running northward for thirty miles was 1,700 pounds sterling and 149 barrels of goods such as axes, bolts of cloth and blankets. A town site was surveyed in the southern part the following year, but nothing happened until John Graves Simcoe, first Governor of Upper Canada, established Fort York in 1793 and designated the future town as the capital of his province. He did not favour the Indian name Toronto, nor did he particularly want to be reminded of the French, and so he named his fort and the settlement "York" after the son of George III of England. At noon on August 27, 1793 he ordered the first royal salute to be fired by the garrison to celebrate the birth of York. Actual building of the town did not begin until the following year. Government House to begin with was a canvas tent until the first Parliament Buildings were constructed at Front and Berkeley Streets. Simcoe and his wife Elizabeth built their residence on a high bluff at the west bank of the Don River. They called it "Castle Frank", and Mrs. Simcoe in her diary tells of the stream being full of salmon which the Indians speared at night. Yonge Street was one of Governor Simcoe's projects. His rangers cut thirty miles of it out of the bush in record time. Today it is the longest main street on this continent.

About a dozen log houses and a handful of hardy pioneers made up the town of York in the early days, and its growth was slow for the first two decades. During the war of

Toronto Harbour in 1803

1812 York made its first mark in international history when it bravely stood up against a force of 2,400 Americans who captured the fort after an eight-hour battle on April 27, 1813, consequently burned the public buildings and temporarily occupied the town.

Built on low-lying, heavy soil, the capital of Upper Canada soon became known as "Muddy York" to the outside world, and a story circulated in those days that someone once picked up a hat on Yonge Street only to find that it belonged to a gentleman sitting on a horse which was stuck in the mud. Nevertheless, York began to grow. Citizens took their turns as fire wardens, constables and poundkeepers. Churches were built, and the first state school opened in 1807 at the corner of King and George Streets. The old Blue School, dating back to 1816, was located at Adelaide and Church.

Inns and taverns were numerous, to say the least. The corner of Queen and Yonge Streets at one time boasted three such flourishing establishments, not to mention the rest of them in and outside of town. The Red Lion Inn, built in 1808 on the east side of Yonge north of Bloor, served its patrons for eighty years. By the middle of the last century there was at least one tavern to every city block.

Toronto's first industrial enterprise of significance was Jesse Ketchum's tannery established in 1812 on the southwest corner of Yonge and Adelaide Streets. Jesse Ketchum owned a great deal of land in the city and, giving away freely of his properties and wealth to worthy causes, he became one of Toronto's early philanthropists. Although a devout Anglican, he sponsored churches of many denominations. He was an ardent fighter for temperance, and at his request at least one street in Toronto was to be kept free of taverns, that was Temperance Street.

Among the first barristers to be appointed to the bar of Upper Canada was Dr. William Warren Baldwin. His name is associated with Spadina Avenue which he planned as the city's most beautiful street; wide and sweeping, lined with trees, it led to his mansion called "Spadina House".

City Hall - 1845

In the early days York was ruled by what was known as the Family Compact. What it meant was that all influential positions were held by members and friends of a few leading families in the province. Bishop Strachan, educator and the first Anglican Bishop of York, was a strong pillar of the Family Compact. His name and work are intimately connected with Toronto's early history. It was the bishop who was instrumental in the founding of King's College, chartered in 1827 as the first institution of higher learning in what is now Ontario. It later was to become the University of Toronto.

In the year 1834 the Town of York ceased to exist and, reverting back to the old Indian name, the City of Toronto was incorporated. The population had reached some 9,000, and the city spread over an area of about one square mile. Northward it had grown to Dundas Street, and its lake front stretched from Bathurst to Parliament Street. William Lyon Mackenzie became the first Mayor of Toronto. A fiery Scotsman, eloquent newspaper editor and passionate fighter for justice, he also was a vigorous opponent of the Family Compact. His colourful career as a reformer climaxed in the armed Rebellion of 1837 of which he was the chief instigator. A battle on December 7th near Montgomery's

Tavern on Yonge Street ended with his defeat. A reward of one thousand pounds on his head, he fled to the United States. Twelve years later, when an amnesty was granted to political offenders, he again returned to Toronto as an honoured citizen. Incidentally, it was Mackenzie who designed the city's coat of arms and gave it its motto: "Industry, Integrity, Intelligence".

For the first decade after Toronto had become a city, part of the old market building served as municipal offices. The brick building with wooden galleries on four sides sheltering the butcher stalls below, once occupied the entire square formed by Front, Jarvis, King and Church Streets. It was not until 1844 that the first city hall was erected on the south side of Front Street between Jarvis and Market Streets. What still exists of this city hall is now part of the south section of the St. Lawrence Market. From here the city fathers conducted their business until in 1899 they moved to Queen Street where a majestic city hall tower rose three hundred feet from the sidewalk. The bells of Big Ben, as it came to be called, rang for the first time on December 31 ushering in a new century of spectacular growth and prosperity for Toronto.

Woven into the tapestry of Toronto's background are the histories of many an old business establishment, still going strong and growing. There is the Gooderham and Worts Distillery dating back to 1832 when they set up a flour mill on Trinity Street. As farmers in those days more often paid with grain rather than money, the company began to make whiskey out of the surplus. It now is probably the oldest existing distillery in Canada.

T. Eaton & Co. - 1869

In 1869, at a time when the city was growing rapidly as a business centre, but buying was still largely a matter of credit, haggling over prices and often barter instead of cash transactions, Timothy Eaton introduced his revolutionary "cash-on-the-spot and one-price for all" method of merchandising. On December 8th of

63

Robert Simpson's Store - 1872

that year he opened his first store on Yonge Street staffed by two men, one woman and a boy. The small place, twenty-four by sixty feet in size, was the beginning of a business that eventually became a part of the Canadian way of life.

Brown Brothers, now primarily engaged in the manufacture and wholesale business of commercial stationery products, was founded in 1846 by Thomas Brown on the present site of the King Edward Hotel. The company is now Toronto's thirteenth oldest business establishment in terms of continuous existence.

An emigrant Scot by the name of Robert Simpson opened his two-storey dry goods store at the corner of Queen and Yonge Streets in 1872. Since then the Robert Simpson Company has grown into a multi-million dollar giant with department stores in the major cities of the country.

Heintzman & Co.

Heintzman, now Canada's leading piano manufacturers, began making his pianos in Toronto back in 1850. Theodore Heintzman started the business in his own home with nothing but his skill and the help of his wife. And then there was Samuel J. Moore of Toronto, founder of the business forms industry, who in 1882 with two steam presses first produced duplicating sales books. Today the Moore Corporation is the largest manufacturer of manifold business forms in the world.

Daniel Massey founded his farm machinery works in Newcastle, Ontario in the year 1847. His son Hart moved the company to Toronto in 1879. It became known under the name Massey-Harris and later Massey-Ferguson as the world's biggest manufacturer of farm machinery, and the story of the company's growth is in part that of Canada's development to one of the most important industrial and agricultural nations on earth.

Eugene O'Keefe was five years old in 1832 when his family emigrated from Ireland and settled in York. Thirty years later he embarked on his career in the brewing business. The corner of Victoria and Gould Streets in Toronto, where he made his fortune, still is the seat of a great brewing organization, and the area with its warehouses, retail store, brewery and office buildings has come to be called the brewing centre of Canada.

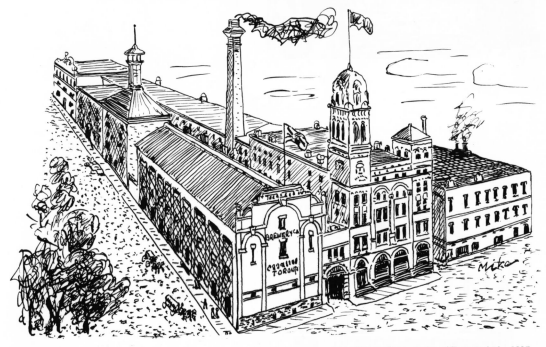

The O'Keefe Brewery Co. of Toronto Ltd. - 1895

The names I have mentioned provide no more than a glimpse at a few of a long list of enterprising citizens who have paved the way in the past for the Toronto we know today. From a trading post in the wilderness they have helped to shape it into a business capital and an industrial giant. A city does not grow, it is built by its people.

King Street East - 1877

Of Enterprise and Prosperity

Metropolitan Toronto is the business heart of a rich and prosperous province. Its heart beat is strong, and its wealth is reflected not only in the giant structures of its many large enterprises, but also in the steady hum of the machinery of nearly five thousand smaller manufacturing plants which are employing a vast number of people and are helping to insure future expansion and prosperity.

Industrial land purchased for expansion in the Toronto area during the last fifteen years would cover a site of nearly fifteen thousand acres. The manufacturing output of greater Toronto surpasses that of any other area of equal size in Canada, so we are told by statistics. Toronto too is a major wholesale distribution centre and the largest retail market in the country. Its annual retail sales have climbed over the two and a half billion dollar mark. It is a place abounding with opportunities for every kind of enterprise. It attracts advertising agencies, manufacturers' agents, engineering and construction firms. Headquarters of leading Canadian corporations, insurance and trust companies, over six hundred branches and several head offices of Canadian chartered banks, they all are part of the bloodstream that keeps Metro Toronto's healthy business heart beating. In terms of "cheques cashed", transactions in Toronto annually come to more than one hundred and fifty billion dollars.

Once every year, since 1879, Toronto has been the scene of the Canadian National Exhibition which has been called the "show window of the nation". As the world's largest annual exhibition it draws some three million visitors and hundreds of exhibitors from across the country.

67

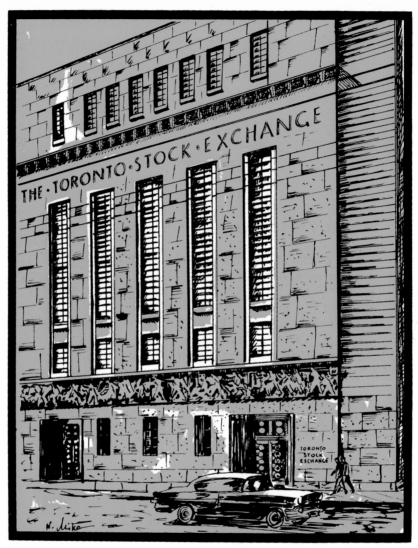

The Toronto Stock Exchange is one of the busiest in the world. Its roots go back to 1852 when a handful of businessmen started getting together every morning to trade their stocks and bonds. Today the market value of stocks listed on the Toronto Exchange is in the neighbourhood of one hundred billion dollars.

Canadian Imperial Bank of Commerce Building

The institution, now known as the Canadian Imperial Bank of Commerce, was formed in 1961 by the merger of two of Canada's oldest chartered banks, the Canadian Bank of Commerce and the Imperial Bank of Canada. It is now one of the world's largest banks.

For more than a quarter century, until the early 1960's, the head office building of the Canadian Bank of Commerce on King Street West in Toronto has held the title of being the tallest structure in the British Commonwealth. With 34 storeys it rises 476 feet above the sidewalk. It has four basements and a depth of 65 feet below street level. From the observation deck of the tower you can enjoy a breathtaking view of the great metropolis below with its highway arteries, its busy harbour and highrise structures. Looking down you realize that the Toronto area is dotted with many parks and that there are a lot of trees mingled in with the forest of steel and concrete. Along the gallery, spaced at intervals, are sixteen giant heads carved in stone, watching over the city below.

William Lyon Mackenzie Building

At the top of Toronto Street on Adelaide East, where once the eighth post office was located, now stands the William Lyon Mackenzie Building which houses among other government departments a postal station and the National Film Board.

Massey-Ferguson Building on University Avenue

The head office of a world-wide organization, known as the Massey-Ferguson Limited, is located in Toronto. It was in 1938 that the then Massey-Harris Company perfected a self-propelled combine which can do the work of no less than three hundred men per day. When in 1953 the company merged with the Ferguson interests, it acquired the revolutionary Ferguson tractor, a light-weight tractor that can perform the work of a machine twice its size. A small farm implement shop, started in Canada by Daniel Massey back in 1847, has grown into an enterprise with manufacturing plants located in every major country. Massey-Ferguson now is the largest maker of tractors, self-propelled combines and diesel engines in the world.

Bank of Nova Scotia

The Bank of Nova Scotia, founded in 1832 by a group of merchants and ship owners gathered at the Exchange Coffee House in Halifax, is now the second oldest surviving bank in Canada with branches across the country and a network of offices throughout the world. The bank's modern executive office building was opened at King and Bay Streets in Toronto in 1951, a location which is known as the "financial crossroads of Canada".

The Shell Building, a handsome twenty-storey structure on University Avenue, was opened in December of 1958. It had only thirteen storeys then, but footings, foundations
and main structure were designed for seven more floors to be added when required.
Now another skyscraper has taken its place among the developments on one of Canada's
most distinguished avenues.

The Canada Life Building

In downtown Toronto you can predict to-morrow's weather simply by looking up into the sky, provided that you know how to read the weather beacon on top of the Canada Life Building. If the light is green, the weather will be clear, flashing red means rain, and flashing white forecasts snow. Lights running up or down the beacon tower indicate warmer or cooler weather respectively. If the light is steady, no change is to be expected.

The well-known landmark at University Avenue and Queen Street is the home office of the Canada Life Assurance Company. One of the older buildings on Toronto's prestige boulevard, the monumental structure was designed by architect R. A. Waite, the man who also was responsible for the Legislative Buildings and the Bank of Commerce.

74

Union Carbide with plants, laboratories and sales offices from coast to coast is one of Canada's major producers of chemicals, resins, gases, metals and carbon, plastic products and consumer products.

The 11-storey head office building of Union Carbide Canada Limited is located on Eglinton Avenue East in Toronto. Opened in 1960, it is one of the most elegant office buildings in the country.

75

North American Life Assurance Company Building

The Head Office Building of the North American Life Assurance Company, located on Adelaide Street West, was officially opened in 1962.

Bata International Centre

In September of 1965 some 250 senior members of the Bata Shoe Organization from over 50 countries gathered in Toronto for the Bata World Conference, traditionally held approximately every three years and for the first time assembled in Canada. This particular conference coincided with the official opening of a striking new building in Flemingdon Park, Toronto, to be known as the Bata International Centre.

With 80 companies, including shoe factories, tanneries, textile mills and rubber plantations, independently operating in 83 countries, the Bata Shoe Organization is the largest manufacturer of footwear in the world. It started out as a small business founded in 1894 by Thomas Bata in a village in Czechoslovakia.

On the northwest corner of King and Bay Streets once stood a small, unpretentious building, formerly a bishop's home. It served as the Bank of Montreal's office back in the years from 1842 to 1845. A little over a century later, in 1949, a modern 16-storey Bank of Montreal building was opened on this very spot. It serves as the bank's main office in Toronto and as headquarters for Ontario.

Toronto-Dominion Centre — Office Tower

The newest of the giants, now dominating the skyline of Toronto, is not only one of the world's tallest buildings, but also one of the most modern structures. It soars 56 storeys to a height of 740 feet, with floor-to-ceiling windows in every office, 32 high-speed computer-programmed passenger elevators, an observation deck offering a panoramic view of the city, and a gourmet restaurant. The tower, now rapidly nearing completion, marks the beginning of one of the most ambitious projects in the heart of the city.

The Toronto-Dominion Centre, as the enterprise is called, will ultimately contain a second 44-storey office tower, and a one-storey elegant banking hall to be erected at the site of the old main branch and head office of the Toronto-Dominion Bank at the southwest corner of King and Bay Streets.

The setting of this development will be an attractively landscaped plaza with fountains, walks and seating areas, two lower levels to be used for parking, and a host of shops, restaurants and service establishments located on the concourse level.

The Toronto-Dominion Centre is estimated to cost 125 million dollars when completed. Its facilities will provide a comfortable and unique business home for thousands of people, and its beauty will enrich the heart of the city.

The Eaton Centre, a project which will mean the re-development of a 20-acre downtown site at an estimated cost of 250 million dollars, is yet in its planning stages. The fate of Toronto's old City Hall is intimately connected with the Centre's gigantic building program that will drastically alter the face of a downtown area and continue the trend towards a new concept in architecture in keeping with Toronto's ultra-modern new City Hall.

A 69-storey apartment and office tower, 910 feet tall, will be part of the Eaton Centre. Rising free of its sister skyscrapers, it will take its place among the giants of the world.

A new Eaton department store and retail complex promises to be one of the largest and most luxurious to be found anywhere. A great gallery, several storeys high, will be occupied by specialty shops, services and other types of retail outlets. Floors will be interconnected by escalators with entrances to the Eaton store on all levels.

Among the buildings that eventually will make up the Eaton Centre is a circular 500-room convention hotel, designed with the most up-to-date facilities, elegant and functional.

Eaton Centre as a whole is planned on a grand and lavish scale. Together with the other gigantic developments now taking shape it will be the core of a new Toronto, and its towering structures will become symbols of Canada's spectacular economic growth.

Eaton-Centre

81

The head office of the Imperial Oil Company is located in a 20-storey building on St. Clair Avenue in Toronto. The oil industry has come a long way since the founders of Imperial Oil pioneered the first refineries in Canada a century ago. There was a time when motorists had to buy their gasoline in buckets from a grocery or hardware store. It was in 1908 that Imperial Oil opened Canada's first service station in Vancouver.

The Simpson Tower

Now rising on Bay Street at the corner of Queen is the 33-storey Simpson Tower. When it is completed, it will feature commercial, shopping and social conveniences that will help to make downtown Toronto an exciting place. The Robert Simpson department store will be accessible from a handsome lobby, banking services will be available on the mezzanine floor, while modern restaurants and cafeterias on the 7th and 8th floors will be capable of serving seventeen hundred people at one sitting.

King Edward Sheraton Hotel

One of the oldest established downtown hotels is the King Edward Sheraton on King Street East. Long a well-known name to travelling Canadians, the hotel has over 800 guest rooms, suites and meeting rooms, and its office and shopping arcade includes the headquarters of Toronto's Convention and Tourist Association. The King Edward is noted among other things for its lavishly designed dining rooms which provide an old-world atmosphere of luxury. One of the hotel's remarkable assets is the fact that it successfully combines Edwardian elegance with modern comfort and facilities.

84

The Royal York Hotel

Jordan's York Hotel, a humble establishment dating back to 1801 and once the most fashionable hotel in Upper Canada, is said to be the ancestor of the Royal York in Toronto which opened in 1929. A far cry from its predecessor, the Royal York with a new 17-storey wing added in 1959, is not only a famous convention centre, but also the largest hotel in the Commonwealth, capable of accommodating as many as 2,400 guests and serving 10,000 people at any one meal.

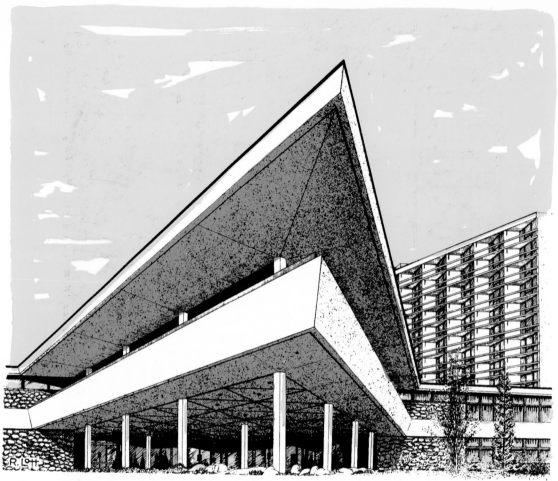

The Inn on the Park

The ultimate in luxury, surrounded by twenty acres of forest and parkland, courtyard gardens with a waterfall and a duck pond, recreational facilities for every taste, a heliport providing helicopter service to the International Airport, gourmet dining and lavish ballrooms, these are some of the attractions that make the Inn on the Park a unique resort hotel in the heart of Metro Toronto. The strikingly designed building is located at Eglinton Avenue and Leslie Street on the edge of the Serena Gundy Park.

Highrise apartment buildings have not only changed the face of many Toronto streets, they have also introduced a new way of life to city dwellers. Attractively landscaped with greenery, fountains and flood-lit pools, they feature doormen, broadloom, elegant lounges, swimming pools, television intercoms, even their own restaurants and boutiques. Luxury is the key note for such developments as the Village Green Apartments.

A 23-storey apartment complex, "The Old Mill Towers", is a new landmark on the western slope of the Humber River valley.

Among the new apartment developments that make up a large portion of Toronto's orbiting construction boom, is the handsome building on Prince Arthur Avenue.

Public Reference Library

John Hallam, a merchant-immigrant from England and a man who very much loved books, is considered the father of the Toronto Public Library. Despite strong objections from some citizens who maintained that public funds should not be used frivolously for the circulation of entertaining books, he helped to bring about the establishment of the Toronto Public Library in 1884 with headquarters located in the Mechanics Institute at the corner of Church and Adelaide Streets. In 1908 a new central library, now known as the Public Reference Library, was erected at College and St. George Streets.

Bell Telephone Building

No. 76 Adelaide Street is the nerve centre of communications in downtown Toronto. From here Bell telephone operators around the clock handle more than 35,000 calls every 24 hours. Here too is located the main control and switching centre for radio and television programs carried over the trans-Canada telephone system's chain of microwave radio-relay stations and cable network.

Consumers' Gas Company Building on Toronto Street

In 1840 a small gas works furnished the first gas lights in the city on an experimental basis. During the following year the Toronto Gas-Light and Water Company was incorporated, and gas became the first public utility in the City of Toronto. Water, incidentally, was not distributed until 1843. A hundred street lamps and a handful of shops were the first gas consumers. Householders still used their tallow candles. Contemporary newspapers called the dimly lighted streets a brilliant spectacle. People began to venture out into the streets at night without fear, and the lamplighter with his long pole on his nightly rounds soon became a familiar sight. The Consumers' Gas Company was formed in 1849 by users of manufactured gas in Toronto. It has served Toronto for 118 years, and since 1955 natural gas has been used throughout the system.

92

On May 2, 1911 a torch-light procession moved from the King Edward Hotel to the old City Hall to mark the event of hydro power being officially turned on in Toronto. Streets no longer were lighted by gas. Toronto Hydro bought power generated at Niagara Falls from Ontario Hydro and distributed it throughout the city. Actually, the first electric arc lights had appeared in Toronto as far back as 1884. But in the early days electricity was available only on a small scale from privately owned companies.

Places of Worship

Toronto has long been known on this continent as the "city of churches". Its people of various ethnic backgrounds and faiths worship in more than twenty different languages in cathedrals of traditional classic design, in humble gospel halls, and in an ever growing number of churches and synagogues of strikingly modern architecture. Among the magnificent old Gothic churches is St. James' Cathedral. Its predecessor was a small wooden structure which occupied the same site in the early 1800's when the congregation of St. James was the first in the town of York.

Little Trinity on King Street East is now the oldest surviving church in the City of

Little Trinity Church - King Street East

Toronto. It was called "the poor man's church" as it was once attended mostly by industrial workers. Under the patronage of Bishop Strachan construction of Trinity Church was started in 1843. For several years the first rector of the church, Reverend W. H. Ripley, served without pay. Gutted by fire in 1961, Little Trinity has been restored and is today a fine example of the early Gothic Revival style.

Church of the Holy Trinity

And there is the Church of the Holy Trinity west of Yonge Street on Trinity Square. It was built in 1847 with the anonymous gift of five thousand pounds from an English lady who as a stranger once visited Toronto and found to her dismay that church pews had to be rented. She asked that her money be used to erect a church in Toronto called Holy Trinity, that the pews be free forever, and that no obstacles should come between the altar and the people. This is one reason why there are no pillars in the Church of the Holy Trinity.

In the early days of York, Roman Catholic services were held in private homes by priests passing through town. It was not until 1826 that the first Catholic Church was built in York. In 1845 Bishop Power, first Roman Catholic Bishop of Toronto, laid the cornerstone of St. Michael's Cathedral. He died before he could see his church completed, labouring for the cholera-stricken during the epidemic of 1847.

Among the many Anglican Churches of Toronto is the Church of the Redeemer at the corner of Bloor Street and Avenue Road. It was built in 1879 replacing an earlier church of the same name which had been moved to this site in 1871. The first Church of the Redeemer actually had started out in the 1840's as St. Paul's, was moved twenty years later to become a Sunday school and chapel-of-ease, and once again changed locations in 1871 when it was called the Church of the Redeemer.

Before it became part of the United Church of Canada the stately Metropolitan Church built in 1870 belonged to the Methodists. Reverend Egerton Ryerson, the father of Upper Canada's educational system, laid the cornerstone. Metropolitan Church is known to possess one of the finest organs in the country. The first Methodist Church of York, incidentally, was erected back in 1818 and stood on King Street West.

St. Andrew's Presbyterian Church at the corner of King and Simcoe Streets was opened in February of 1876. Its picturesque design was influenced by the architectural style of the old kirks in Scotland. The first minister of the church was Reverend D. J. Macdonnell who previously served at the mother church, the original St. Andrew's, a plain brick structure which was built in 1831 and once stood at the corner of Church and Adelaide Streets.

The Mirrors of Toronto

Browsing through newspapers of by-gone days can be a fascinating hobby. Want and sales ads tell a story all their own about life in the "good old days", when Dr. Brandreth's blood purifying pills promised to prevent sickness, and employers searched for persons harbouring run-away apprentices to be dealt with by the law. Newspapers of yesterday are the mirrors of history. They record events, reflect opinions of their time and portray life in its every-day aspects. Susannah Moodie, wellknown author of books on pioneer life in Canada, described the Canadian newspapers of a hundred years ago as "a strange melange of politics, religion, abuse and general information".

The first paper to appear in Toronto, and the only one for two decades, was the "Upper Canada Gazette or American Oracle", an official publication originally established in Newark by Governor Simcoe in 1793 and transplanted to York on October 4, 1798.

Before Confederation in 1867, Toronto saw over eighty different newspapers come and go. The first unofficial paper was the "Observer" which appeared on May 22, 1820. In those days editors expressed their own convictions freely and vigorously fought for what they believed to be right. The most colourful and outspoken of them all was William Lyon Mackenzie, publisher of the "Colonial Advocate". He fought the powerful Family Compact rule of his day on the pages of his paper and never was one for mincing his words. One day some of his opponents smashed his printing press and threw the type into Toronto Bay. Mackenzie not only won 625 pounds in damages, but is credited with publishing the first diagram of the route taken by the attackers ever to appear in a newspaper.

"The Loyalist" was a strong supporter of the Family Compact in 1828 but the paper lived only for about a year as did many others in the old days. There were semi-weeklies such as "The Courier of Upper Canada" which started in 1829, and the "Toronto Morning Visitor" published twice a week in 1835 bringing the latest European and Provincial news. September 10, 1835 was the date when the one and only issue of "The Porcupine" appeared. "The Examiner", established in 1838, was fighting for responsible government. In the 1850's and '60's it was "The Grumbler", a humorous political weekly and its equally sharp oponent, "The Poker". Before the turn of the last century there was a period when Toronto was a city with seven daily papers. Two of them appeared in the morning as well as in the evening, making it a total of nine newspapers to read.

Today there are three Toronto dailies, "The Globe and Mail", "The Telegram", and the "Toronto Daily Star", all of them rated as influential newspapers throughout the country with a wide circulation. Toronto, too, is the seat of Canada's largest publishing house, the "Maclean-Hunter Publishing Company", with over forty business papers, magazines and news publications. Toronto is the headquarters of national press organizations and the seat of most major publishers. But it is not only the city of the printed word, it is also a capital of radio and television, the communications media of our century.

"The Globe and Mail" today is Canada's largest morning newspaper. It was on March 5, 1844 that George Brown, a Scottish immigrant and one of the Fathers of Confederation, founded the Globe as a weekly in Toronto. The first issue of the Globe consisted of three hundred copies, but within ten years of its existence it had a circulation of more than ten thousand, and on October 1, 1853 it became a daily paper.

In 1936 a former Globe employee, George McCullagh in association with William H. Wright bought the Globe. A few weeks later he announced that the Globe had absorbed "The Mail and Empire", and on November 23, 1936 the paper appeared for the first time as "The Globe and Mail".

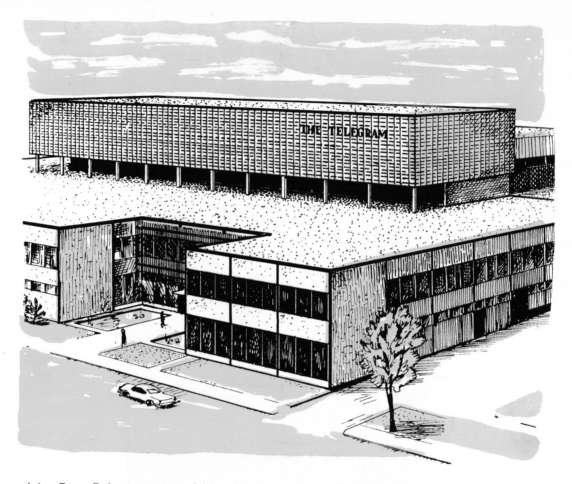

John Ross Robertson started his career as a journalist while he was still at school. He published "The Daily Telegraph", Toronto's first evening paper, in 1866 and ten years later he became the founder of "The Evening Telegram". The first issue of the highly successful paper appeared on April 18, 1876. The old Telegram building that stood at the corner of Bay and Melinda Streets was once considered the most modern newspaper building on the continent. People used to crowd the street in front of the premises every afternoon eagerly awaiting the 5 o'clock edition of the Telegram. The new building on Front Street West opened in 1963 once more can claim the fame of being one of the most modern newspaper plants in existence.

The "Toronto Daily Star", youngest of the three surviving, long established papers in Toronto, began its life as "The Evening Star". The first issue appeared on November 3, 1892, but the paper did not really flourish until a few years later. It was vigorous Joseph E. Atkinson, editor, publisher and later owner of the Star, who in 1899 launched the paper on its spectacular career. He also started the "Toronto Star Weekly" which first appeared in April of 1910. It was an equally successful venture, and not only did the Star Weekly overtake its competitor, "The Toronto Sunday World", it absorbed it, and in terms of circulation became one of Toronto's largest publications.

CBC's Radio Building and Television Studios

Radio came to Toronto in the early 1920's, a time when privately owned stations began to spring up all over the country. Operating on very low power, Canadian stations during their first decade reached only about half the population, national programming was extremely limited because of costly distribution, and interference from the more powerful American stations was a constant problem. In 1936 the Canadian Broadcasting Corporation was created, its main objectives being to make it possible for every Canadian to hear Canadian programs and to provide the best possible from every available source. Toronto's first television station, CBLT, was opened on September 8, 1952.

From Steam Era to Jet Age

In the days before trains and automobiles it was the stage coach that carried freight and passengers. A journey over the deeply rutted roads was more likely to be a nightmare than a pleasure. To travel from Toronto to Hamilton took a whole day provided nothing happened.

Birch canoes, bateaux and Durham boats once were the means of transportation on water. Horse-boats with paddle-wheels were used as ferries. One of them, "The Packet",

Steamer "City of Toronto"

still operated in the Toronto harbour at the middle of the last century. In the 1820's seven steamships regularly plied the waters of Lake Ontario. The first mail steamer coming into York harbour was the "Canada". Also calling at York in the early days of steamboats was the "Frontenac", once considered as comfortable as a luxury hotel steaming along at ten miles per hour. Among the many famous steamships that once plied the Lake was the "City of Toronto", regularly sailing between Toronto and Niagara from 1841 to 1863.

Steam Engine "Toronto"

And then came the Iron Horse, the steam locomotive which opened up a whole new way of life and started the wheels of progress rolling. The first steam engine to be built in Canada came from Good's Foundry in Toronto. It had been ordered by the Ontario, Simcoe and Huron line, also known as the Oats, Straw and Hay Railway, and later to become the Northern Railway of Canada. On April 16, 1853 the quaint little steam engine, named "Toronto" after the city of her origin, with her impressive smokestack belching clouds of black smoke, made her way down Yonge Street to her permanent tracks on Front Street at the foot of Bay. It was slow going because every so often a section of the rails had to be lifted behind her and again placed ahead of her as she moved past the awe-struck spectators lining the street. Exactly one month later, on

May 16th, she headed the first train ever to run in Ontario. Consisting of four yellow-painted passenger cars carrying dignitaries in high hats and ladies in their Sunday-best, the train left Toronto for Machell's Corners, now known as Aurora. The historic event is commemorated by a plaque at the entrance of Toronto's Union Station.

October 27, 1856 was another memorable day in Toronto's railway history. It was the day, when the first through train from Montreal arrived in Toronto on the newly completed Grand Trunk line. In those days trains ran on local time, and clocks were twenty-three minutes slower in Toronto than they were in Montreal. Incidentally, it was a Toronto citizen, Sir Sanford Fleming, who some twenty years later invented Standard Time

Union Station

which was adopted by most countries in the world, putting an end to a lot of confusion for travellers.

The first Union Station in Toronto was built for the joint use of the Grand Trunk, the Northern and the Great Western Railways. Passengers arrived at a little brick building at the foot of York Street until a new and more up-to-date station was erected in 1873 west of York Street. The present Union Station was begun in 1914, but it was not until thirteen years later that it was officially opened by the Prince of Wales. Somewhat outdated now as modern stations go, it too will likely be replaced some day in the not too distant future, but it has seen millions of passengers arrive and depart over the years and has seen Toronto become one of the busiest terminals in the country. At least 125 freight trains arrive or depart Toronto each day. Giant new freight classification yards in the suburbs, equipped with radar and computers, sort, assemble and dispatch the trains that carry goods of every description to and from the great industrial centre.

In May of 1840 the schooner "Fly" left the wharf of Gooderham and Worts in Toronto to sail for Montreal. The vessel was carrying the first recorded shipment of manufactured goods from Upper Canada. Today ocean freighters from most of the world's shipping lines come to the port of Toronto. Since the opening of the St. Lawrence Seaway in 1959 Toronto's spacious harbour has become one of the busiest on the Great Lakes and a gateway to the world's markets. Over a million tons of ocean-going cargo are loaded and unloaded in Toronto per year in addition to the more than five million tons carried to and from the port by Great Lake freighters. Administered by the Toronto Harbour Commission, the harbour has expanded over an area of more than two thousand acres with seventeen new acres being reclaimed each year from Lake Ontario and added to the port's facilities.

When Toronto became a city in 1834, parking space was no problem for the citizens, all you needed was a hitching post. Streets were dust in the summer, mud and slush most any other time of the year, and the wooden sidewalks built in the 1830's were much appreciated by the ladies in their long, sweeping skirts. A few years later most street centres were either paved or macadamized, although the latter process often meant no more than a load of stone spread loosely over the muddy surface. Then came pavement consisting of cedar blocks, and during the 1880's asphalt made its first appearance on Toronto streets.

The year 1849 saw the first public transportation service inaugurated in Toronto. It consisted of four six-passenger omnibuses operated by a cabinet maker between the St. Lawrence Market via King and Yonge Streets to the Red Lion Hotel north of Bloor. In September of 1861 Torontonians took their first streetcar ride. Drawn by horses, the car was derailed twice on its maiden run along Yonge Street, but the enthusiastic crowd helped to lift it back onto the tracks. During the winter passengers' feet were

Ships loading at Toronto Harbour

kept warm by a bundle of straw. The Street Railway Company had the snow shovelled onto the sidewalk while shopkeepers on Yonge Street angrily shovelled it right back onto the tracks. Electric trolleys first ran in 1892 on Church Street, flying along like "demons" at the break-neck speed of ten miles per hour leaving bewildered pedestrians and horses all along the route. Next on the scene was the horse-less carriage, the miracle of all inventions. Electric, steam-driven and gasoline-powered automobiles began to appear on Toronto streets, and things have never been the same since. Those were the good old days, when Henry Ford sold his "Tin Lizzie" for less than three hundred dollars.

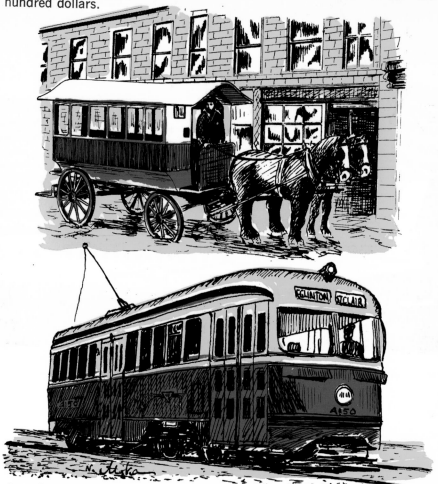

Toronto's public transit system today is a far cry from the cabinet makers omnibus service, but then so is the volume of traffic. To cope with the hundred thousands of passengers that move about the metropolitan area every day, a significant part of transportation has gone underground. The subway-rider has no parking problems, trains are speedy and comfortable and when expansions to the existing lines are completed in 1967, Toronto will have a subway system second to none.

Every five minutes, day and night, one aircraft takes off or lands at Toronto International Airport. In excess of three million passengers every year make use of its ultra-modern facilities. Airlines from all over the world come to Toronto International Airport, and while it handles the giant long-range jet liners, the busy Toronto Island Airport looks after the lighter medium-sized planes and has developed into one of the largest seaplane bases in the country. Both airports were built in 1938. Malton, as the International Airport was known for some time, had two 3000-foot runways, and the administration building then consisted of an old farmhouse which stood on the property. At the outbreak of World War II, Malton became an important training base. Aircraft industries moved into the area around the airport, and following the advent of jet and supersonic flight, it quickly began to take on a new look as preparations were made to cope with the rapid advances in aviation technology. Today its striking and unusual terminal building with circular aeroquay and service facilities second to none, make it one of the most modern and attractive airports in Canada.

A Stroll through Toronto

Some people explore a city with the help of a tourist guide book. Others take a sight-seeing trip in a comfortable bus. No doubt, they see most of what there is to see — the impressive buildings, a few historic landmarks, the glittering stores along the main thoroughfares. But what they are not likely to find are the little curiosities that make up the character of a city. Besides they miss the sense of adventure that comes with discovering on their own what a city is like, strolling around, talking to people,

Nathan Phillips Square

115

Central Firehall

asking questions. An old-timer sitting on a bench in a Toronto park will tell you quite a bit about the city as it used to be.

If you merely want to watch people, Nathan Phillips Square is the place to go. The Indian word "Toronto" means "Place of Meeting", and this is what the city's huge civic square in front of the new city hall has become. Even more in the wintertime when throngs of spectators watch the hundreds of skaters glide over the artificially frozen surface of the pool whose fountains spout twelve thousand gallons of water per minute during the hot summer months. An added feature that draws crowds to the square is Henry Moore's "Archer", the abstract bronze sculpture that recently has taken its place in front of City Hall.

What is left of Chinatown, just north of City Hall, is a colourful neighbourhood at any time to a stranger. But on a Sunday morning it might turn out to be even more interesting than eating Chinese food. The last time I took a walk along Dundas Street behind City Hall, I saw a dragon dance and people jump when a dozen firecrackers exploded. I wondered why from each window dangled a rope to which bits of lettuce leaves and dollar bills were tied. Mind you, the money was just high enough above one's head to be tempting. Grocery stores in Chinatown were open that Sunday morning, and housewives were buying fresh beansprouts. Crates were piled on the sidewalk stencilled "Hong-Kong". A man wheeled a cart with a pail full of something that looked like cottage cheese.

Later that day I watched a veterans' parade led by a band of Scottish pipers, and a group of teenagers, wildly dressed, riding in open convertibles along Avenue Road, soliciting support for the United Appeal. At a corner gas station some dog-lovers paraded their pets up and down, and everyone was dressed up, including the dogs. A car accident caused a traffic jam, and I decided that I had seen enough for one day.

The next time I came to Toronto was on a Saturday. I joined the throngs of Italians, Germans, Ukrainians and a lot of other Torontonians who are in the habit of shopping on Saturday morning at the old St. Lawrence Market. Here Russian babushkas with scarfs over their hair and elegant matrons in mink rub elbows at the butcher stalls laden with sausages that have an old-world flavour. Across the street the hall is filled with the fragrance of farm-fresh vegetables and the shouting of a dozen vendors anxious to sell their produce. Once a week the ancient market comes to life with an atmosphere that the supermarket can never match.

Schoolhouse · 1848

If you are in the neighbourhood of the old city hall, don't forget to take a look at the magnificent stained glass window in the main corridor. It might not be there much longer, as the days of the city hall at the head of Bay Street are numbered. Created by Robert McCausland of Toronto in 1899, the window is a masterpiece in design and colour depicting the

Lighthouse - Lakeshore Boulevard

"Union of Commerce and Industry" and symbolizing the city's development, its trade with the Orient and Occident and its importance as a great port.

There is a section downtown where you will find street signs that read "1793 - Town of York" just above the street's name. It is the area within the boundaries of Ontario Street on the east, George Street on the west, Front on the south, and Adelaide on the north. This location was the site of the original town of York. It is the core around which the great Metropolis was built. Incidentally, in those days the town consisted of about a dozen houses.

Jarvis Street, so people will tell you, is one of the oldest streets in Toronto and once was the most elegant residential street in town. Some of the stately mansions are still there to prove it. But then it deteriorated, and eventually it became known as the "street of sin" with flop houses, wicked women, policemen patrolling in pairs and a paddy wagon always ready just around the corner. Today, however, Jarvis Street on the surface seems to be as respectable as any other busy thoroughfare in Toronto.

Occasionally downtown you can see a policeman mounted on his well-groomed horse, trotting along and keeping an eye on things. He seems to belong to another era, and somehow he makes me want to slow down and forget that I am in a hurry.

Perhaps you like to stop and have a chat with the firemen at the firehall on Lombard Street. They will tell you that their picturesque building is the Central Firehall erected in 1886. If you want to know more about the history of the fire department, you find out that in the days of the hand pumper at least two hundred volunteers were needed to operate this contraption, and that at the time Toronto became a city householders still were required to keep a bucket outside their houses to assist firefighters.

Wandering around you might accidentally discover the little schoolhouse behind Toronto's oldest existing church on King Street. Above the narrow doorway you can still read that it was "erected by Enoch Turner A.D. 1848". What a difference when you compare it to some of the public schools of more recent vintage. If you are interested in church architecture, Toronto is the place to explore. It is called the "city of churches".

Statue of Edward Hanlan

Of course, the old lighthouse would be pointed out by most guides on a sight-seeing bus that happened to pass it on Lakeshore Boulevard. A long time ago it guarded the western gap of Toronto harbour. Today it looks down on the traffic that swirls around it on one of the busiest boule-

119

Bargain Benny's

vards of the city. Speaking of lighthouses, there is another lighthouse, the oldest one on the Great Lakes, which still stands on Toronto Island. Built during the early 1800's, its tapered tower is eighty-two feet in height, and its light in the old days was fed by two hundred gallons of whale oil a year. For nearly a century and a half it guarded the entrance to the harbour and guided the ships sailing the Great Lakes.

The life-like statue of Edward Hanlan you are sure to admire when you stroll through Exhibition Park. If by any chance you don't know who "Ned" Hanlan was, ask any native Torontonian. He will tell you that, aside from being a Toronto Island boy, he was the world's greatest oarsman three quarters of a century ago. At twenty-two he became champion sculler of Canada and three years later champion of the world. As Toronto's first great sports hero, he heads a long list of world renowned athletes the

Huron Street

city has called its own in the years that followed. Torontonians, I found, are quite enthusiastic when it comes to sports.

I also found Torontonians to be friendly people. Most of them anyway. There was the little incident of the streetcar driver stopping and patiently waiting with a big grin on his face while I tried to turn my car around. And what amazed me most was the fact that no one lined up behind him lost his patience either. Who says that no one has time in Toronto?

In Yorkville I met a man who supplements his old-age pension collecting bottles thrown on the street by thoughtless people. He worries that nowadays so many bottles are "not refundable". He too is part of the Toronto scene. So are the chauffeur-driven limousines, the swanky homes in Forest Hill, and the drab, broken-down tenement houses in other sections. Often you see rows of look-alike houses with verandahs, gables and gingerbread trim, survivors of another era. If they are dressed up with a coat of red paint and a postage-stamp-size garden in front, they make for a far more picturesque neighbourhood than some of their modernized contemporaries. Just walk along Soho Street, Sherbourne or Parliament and see for yourself. Sometimes you may need a little imagination to picture their graceful past underneath the peeling paint.

Once I took my father-in-law, who was visiting from Europe, through the east end of Toronto along the four-mile stretch of Danforth Avenue. He tried to count the used-car lots lining the street, but soon gave up somewhat bewildered. Never in his life had he seen anything like this! Danforth, of course, is the mecca of used-car buyers with its thousands of highly polished automobiles, dazzling lights and flashing advertising displays. At night it looks more like a giant midway rather than the home of Canada's largest used-car market. On this stretch of Danforth the yearly business turnover amounts to millions of dollars and customers are liable to come from any part of the country.

Sherbourne Street

When it comes to eye-catching advertisements, Bargain Benny's at the corner of Queen Street and Spadina spares neither splash, paint nor words. Not only is the façade of the old Victorian building literally covered with signs and slogans, you can also read them in any language you happen to speak.

If you like a change of scenery and want to get away from the hustle and bustle of the city for a while, take a walk through Edward Gardens, once part of a farm belonging to an early settler. Its last owner sold the 27-acre estate to the Metro Parks Commission and helped transform it into one of Toronto's loveliest parks. Wilket Creek, spanned by rustic bridges, winds its way through a pleasant valley with little ponds, nature trails, wooded slopes and pretty rock gardens.

Overlooking the valley of the Humber in west Toronto is the famous Old Mill Restaurant. Here you can dine in an old-world atmosphere and enjoy a display of antiques and interesting relics of the past. On the grounds stood once an early grist mill which ground the grain for the settlers in the Humber valley. Its history goes back to the year 1798. The last mill which occupied the historic site was erected in 1849. In the winter of 1881 the building was gutted by fire leaving only the heavy stone walls of the structure. They can still be seen as a monument to the Humber pioneers.

Ruins of Old Mill

Black Creek Pioneer Village

A visit to Pioneer Village at the northern fringe of Metro Toronto takes you back a hundred years and more in history. Here a blacksmith shoes horses, women bake bread in the community oven, and an old grist mill grinds the flour. If it were not for the many visitors who come to Black Creek Pioneer Village to get a glimpse at the past, you would think it was a real live community with a village inn, a one-room schoolhouse and a church serving the farmers and shopkeepers living there.

Well, by now you might want to explore Toronto alone. Find out what a thrill it can be to discover on your own one of the most fascinating cities in Canada.

Index

Adelaide St., 91
airports, 113
Anglican Churches, 98
apartment buildings, 87, 89
"Archer", 6, 116
Arms of the City of Toronto, 56
Art Gallery of Toronto, 50
Atkinson College, 39
Atkinson, Joseph, E., 105
automobiles, 111, 112
Baldwin, Dr. William Warren, 62
Bank of Montreal, 55, 78
Bank of Nova Scotia, 72
Bank of Toronto, 30
Bargain Benny's, 122
Bata International Centre, 77
Bata Shoe Organization, 77
Bata, Thomas, 77
Bay Street, 11, 15
Bell Telephone Co., 91
Black Creek Pioneer Village, 124
Bloor St., 7, 9
Boulton, William, Henry, 50
Brown Brothers, 64
Brown, George, 103
Brown, Thomas, 64
Brûlé, Etienne, 59
Cabbagetown, 32
"Canada", steamship, 108
Canada Life Assurance Co., 74
Canadian Broadcasting Corporation, 106
Canadian Imperial Bank of Commerce, 69, 70
Canadian National Exhibition, 8, 23, 67
Casa Loma, 8, 22
Castle Frank, 60
Catholic churches, 97
CBLT, TV-station, 106
Chinatown, 12, 116
churches, 11, 95
Church of the Redeemer, 98
City Hall, 12, 13, 17, 63, 80
City Hall, stained glass window, 117
City of Toronto, 62
"City of Toronto", steamship, 108
Coat of Arms, 63
Colborne Lodge, 52
Colonnade, 9, 27
"Colonial Advocate", 101
Connaught Medical Research Laboratories, 44
Consumers' Gas Co., 92
Daily Telegraph, The, 104
Danforth Ave., 122
Eaton's, 9, 11, 80
Eaton Centre, 80, 81
Eaton, Timothy, 31, 63
Education Centre, 45, 46
Edward Gardens, 123
electric lights, 93
Evening Star, The, 105
Evening Telegram, The, 104
Examiner, The, 101
Exhibition Park, 48, 53, 60
Family Compact, 62, 101
firehall, 119
Fleming, Sir Sanford, 109
"Fly", schooner, 110
Forest Hill, 122
Fort Rouillé, 48, 59

Fort Toronto, 48, 60
Fort York, 8, 18, 47, 48, 60
gas station, first, 82
Gas Works, 92
Glendon College, 39
Globe, The, 103
Globe and Mail, The, 102, 103
Good's Foundry, 108
Gooderham building, 30
Gooderham & Worts, 30, 63, 110
Government House, 60
Grand Trunk Railways, 52, 109
Grange, 50
Grumbler, The, 101
Hallam, John, 90
Hanlan, Edward, 120
Harbour, 11, 52, 110
Hart House, 38
Heintzman & Co., 64
Heintzman, Theodore, 64
High Park, 8, 52
Holy Trinity Church, 8, 96
Honest Ed, 9, 29
Howard, John, George, 52
Imperial Oil Co., 82
Inn on the Park, 86
inns, 61
International Airport, 113
Island Airport, 113
Jarvis St., 118
Jordan's York Hotel, 85
Juvenile and Family Court Building, 33
Kensington Market, 8
Ketchum, Jesse, 31, 61
King Edward Sheraton Hotel, 84
King Street, 52, 66
lakefront, 12
Lansdowne Public School, 42
lighthouses, 119, 120
Lind, Jenny, 51
Lord Elgin, 50
Lot St., 32
Loyalist, The, 101
Mace of Upper Canada, 48
Mackenzie House, Bond St., 49, 62
Mackenzie, William, Lyon, 49, 63, 101
Maclean-Hunter Publishing Co., 102
Mail and Empire, The, 103
Malton Airport, 113
Maple Leaf Gardens, 9, 20
Markham Village, 9, 29
Massey, Daniel, 65
Massey-Ferguson, 65
Massey, Hart, A., 24
Massey Music Hall, 24
Marine Museum, 53
market, 51
market building, 63
mayor, first, 62
McCausland, Robert, 117
McCullagh, George, 103
Methodist Church, first, 99
Metropolitan Church, 99
Mirvish, Edwin, 26, 29
Montgomery's Tavern, 62
Moodie, Susannah, 101
Moore, Henry, 6, 116
Moore, Samuel J., 64

Index

Mulock, Cawthra, 26
Nathan Phillips Square, 116
newspapers, 101
North American Life Assurance, 76
Observer, 101
O'Keefe Brewery, 65
O'Keefe Centre, 9, 24, 25
Old Mill, 123
Old Mill Towers, 88
omnibus service, first, 110
Ontario House, 30
Ontario Hydro, 93
Ontario, Simcoe and Huron Railway, 108
Osgoode Hall, 34, 35
Osgoode, William, 35
Packet, ferry, 107
Parliament Buildings, 15, 19, 60
Parliament St., 122
Parks, 8
Pellatt, Sir Henry, 22
Pioneer Village, 124
Poker, The, 101
Porcupine, The, 101
Power, Bishop, 97
Princes' Gate, 23
Provincial Archives, 41
Public Library, 90
Queen's Park, 15
Queen St., 32
Radio, 106
railways, 109
Rebellion of 1837, 62
Red Lion Inn, 61
Robertson, John, Ross, 104
Royal Alexandra, 9, 26
Royal Ontario Museum, 43
Royal Winterfair, 23
Ryerson, Rev. Egerton, 99
Scadding Cabin, 48
Scadding, Henry, 48
Scarborough College, 40
schools, 45, 61, 119
Shell building, 73
Sherbourne St., 122
sidewalks, 52
Sigmund Samuel Canadiana Gallery, 41
Simcoe, John, Graves, 18, 47, 59, 60, 101
Simpson's, 9, 83
Simpson, Robert, 31, 64
Simpson Tower, 11, 83
Soho St., 122
Soldier's Tower, 38
Spadina Ave., 8, 62
St. Andrew's Presbyterian Church, 100

St. James' Cathedral, 95
St. James' Cemetery, 52
St. Lawrence Hall, 51
St. Lawrence Market, 51, 63, 117
St. Michael's Cathedral, 97
St. Paul's Church, 98
Standard Time, 109
Stanley Barracks, 53
steamboats, 107, 108
Stock Exchange, 11, 68
streets, 110
street lighting, 92
street railway, 31, 110, 111
subway, 10, 112
Sunnyside Amusement Park, 12
taverns, 61
Telegram, The, 102, 104
Temperance Street, 62
Toronto Daily Star, 102, 105
Toronto-Dominion Bank, 80
Toronto-Dominion Centre, 11, 16, 79, 80
Toronto Gas-Light and Water Co., 92
Toronto Harbour Commission, 110
Toronto Hydro, 93
Toronto Morning Visitor, 101
Toronto Purchase, 60
"Toronto", steam engine, 108
Toronto Star Weekly, 105
Toronto St., 54
Toronto Sunday World, The, 105
Toronto Symphony Orchestra, 24
Town of York, 62, 118
trains, 109
transportation, 10, 31, 110, 112
trolleys, 111
Turner, Enoch, 119
Union Carbide Canada Limited, 75
Union Station, 109, 110
University Ave., 15
University College, 36, 37
University of Toronto, 37
Upper Canada Gazette, 101
Village Green Apartments, 87
Waite, R. A., 74
waterfront, 16
Wellington Hotel, 30
Woodbine Racetrack, 21
Yonge St., 31, 60
York, town, 60, 61
York, Battle of, 47, 61
York Pioneer and Historical Society, 48
York St., 110
York University, 39
Yorkdale, 9
Yorkville, 8, 28

Illustrations

	Page
"Archer", sculpture by Henry Moore	6
Archives Building of the Province of Ontario	41
Arms of the City of Toronto	57
Bank of Montreal, Ontario headquarters	78
Bank of Montreal, Front and Yonge Streets	55
Bank of Nova Scotia	72
Bargain Benny's	120
Bata International Centre	77
Bay Street	15
Bell Telephone Building	91
Canada Life Building	74
Canadian Imperial Bank of Commerce, overlooking city from observation tower	2
Canadian Imperial Bank of Commerce Building	69
Canadian National Exhibition	67
Casa Loma	22
C.B.C. Studio	106
Church of the Holy Trinity	96
Church of the Redeemer	98
City Hall - 1845	62
City Hall at the head of Bay Street	17
City Hall, new	13
"City of Toronto", steamboat	107
Colborne Lodge	52
Colonnade	27
Consumers' Gas Co. - Toronto Street	92
Court House	34
Eaton Centre	81
Eaton Co. - 1869	63
Education Centre	45
Firehall, Central	116
Fort Rouille	59
Fort Rouille - obelisk in Exhibition Park	60
Fort York	47
Globe and Mail Building	103
Gooderham Building, Front and Wellington Streets	30
Grange	50
Hanlan, Edward, statue of	119
Harbour - 1803	61
Hart House	38
Heintzman & Co.	64
Huron Street	121
Hydro Building	93
Imperial Oil Building	82
Inn-on-the-Park	86
Juvenile and Family Court	33
King Edward Hotel	84
King Street East - 1877	66
Lansdowne Public School	42
Library, Central	90
Lighthouse, Lakeshore Blvd.	118
Little Trinity Church	95
Mackenzie Building	70
Mackenzie House, Bond Street	49
Maple Leaf Gardens	20
Map of Toronto	125
Marine Museum	53
Markham Village	29
Massey-Ferguson Building	71
Massey Hall	24
Metropolitan Church	99
Nathan Phillips Square	115
North American Life Building	76
O'Keefe Brewery Co. - 1895	65
O'Keefe Centre	25
Old Mill	123
Old Mill Towers	88
Osgoode Hall	35
Parliament Buildings	19
Pioneer Village	124
Prince Arthur Ave. Apartments	89
Princes' Gate	23
Queen Street	32
Royal Alexandra	26
Royal Ontario Museum	43
Royal York Hotel	85
Scadding Cabin	48
Scarborough College	40
Schoolhouse - 1848	117
Shell Building	73
Sherbourne Street	122
Ships loading at harbour	111
Simcoe, Monument in Queen's Park	18
Simpson Tower	83
Skyline at night	16
St. Andrew's Presbyterian Church	100
St. Lawrence Hall	51
St. Michael's Cathedral	97
Stock Exchange	68
Streetcars	112
Telegram Building	104
Toronto-Dominion Centre	79
Toronto International Airport	113
Toronto Star Building	105
"Toronto", steam locomotive	108
Toronto Street, No. 10	54
Union Carbide Building	75
University College	37
University College, Main Entrance	36
Union Station	109
Village Green Apartments	87
Woodbine Race Track	21
Yonge Street	31
York University	39
Yorkville Village	28